STRING QUARTETS
Nos. 1 and 2

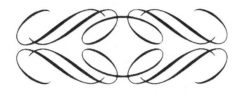

BÉLA BARTÓK

DOVER PUBLICATIONS, INC.
Mineola, New York

Bibliographical Note

This Dover edition, first published in 2004, is a new compilation of two works originally published separately as *1. Quatuor à Cordes / Op. 7 (1908)*, Rózsavölgyi & Cie., Budapest and Leipzig, 1911 [Pl. no.: R. & Co. 3287] and *II. Streichquartett / für 2 Violinen, Viola und Violoncell von Béla Bártok / Op. 17 / Partitur*, Universal-Edition, Vienna, 1920 [Pl. no.: U.E. 6371]. The publisher is grateful to the Sibley Music Library, Eastman School of Music, for the loan of the rare first edition of Quartet No. 1.

International Standard Book Number

ISBN-13: 978-0-486-43799-6
ISBN-10: 0-486-43799-X

Manufactured in the United States by LSC Communications
43799X03   2017
www.doverpublications.com

CONTENTS

String Quartet no. 1, op. 7 (1908–9)

String Quartet no. 2, op. 17 (1914–17)

BÉLA BARTÓK

1. QUATUOR À CORDES

OP. 7 (1908)

PROPRIÉTÉ DES EDITEURS.

RÓZSAVÖLGYI & Cie.

EDITEURS DE MUSIQUE

BUDAPEST et LEIPZIC

NOTE ON THIS EDITION

The present score is an unaltered reprint of the first edition, exactly as it was published by Rózsavölgyi & Cie. in 1911. The original Hungarian title *1. Vonósnégyes* ("1st string quartet") has been retained on the first score page.

Much later in his life, having grown discontented with the tempo indications in many of his early works, Bartók disavowed the tempi in this first edition and outlined revisions, which after his death were incorporated into a new edition of the score. Those revisions consisted in great part of assigning explicit metronome markings to many subtle fluctuations of tempo that the present notation leaves to the discretion of the performer. In the instances where Bartók called for an alteration of existing metronome markings, the revised tempi were invariably faster than the originals; in some places quite dramatically so, particularly in the first and third movements.

Most notable among those changes were the increase from ♪ = 50 to ♪ = 60 (56–63) at the opening of the first movement (later markings in the movement are as fast as ♪ = 72); and the increase from ♩ = 84 to ♩ = 108 at rehearsal [11] in the third movement, beyond which point the music in the revised edition is almost entirely marked 10–20 beats per minute faster than in this first edition.

1. Vonósnégyes.

I.

Bartók Béla
Op. 7. (1908)

3

6

8

II.

10

12

14

15

16

18

19

20

III.

Allegro vivace. ($\bm{\downarrow}$ = 88-92)

23

24

28

32

34

36

Au Quatuor Hongrois Waldbauer, Temesváry,
Kornstein, Kerpely.

II. STREICHQUARTETT

FÜR 2 VIOLINEN, VIOLA UND VIOLONCELL VON

BÉLA BARTÓK

OP. 17

PARTITUR

UNIVERSAL-EDITION WIEN

Au Quatuor Hongrois Waldbauer, Temesváry, Kornstein, Kerpely.

IIeme QUATUOR

I.

Moderato. (♩.= 60 - 56)

Béla Bartók, Op. 17.

44

46

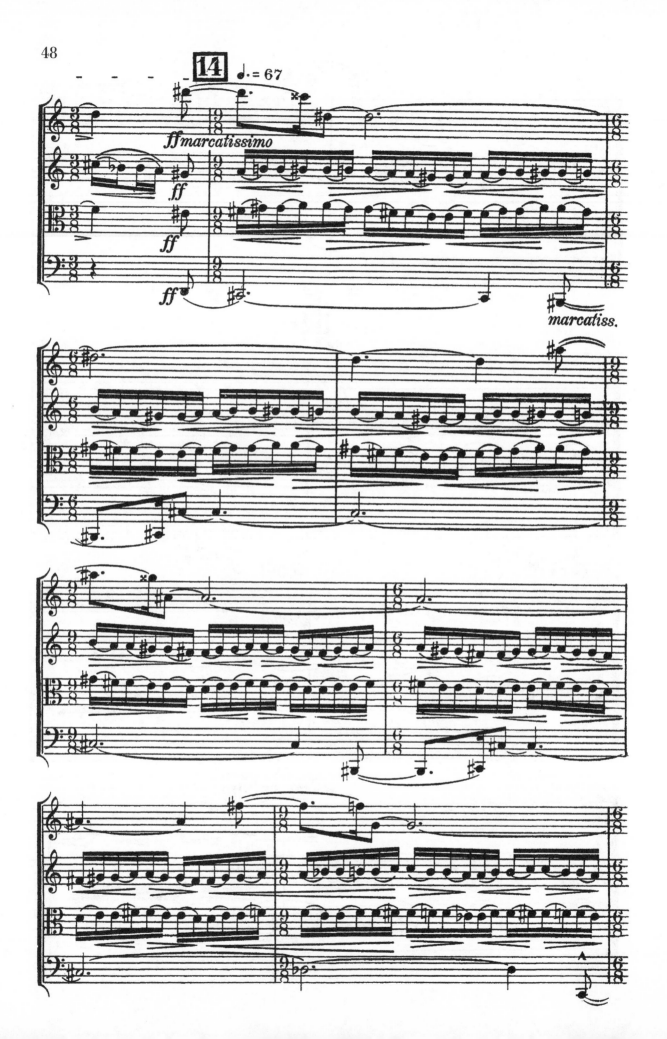

52

56

II.

58

60

66

Allmählicher Übergang von ²/₄ zu ³/₄.
Fokozatos átmenet 2/4-ről 3/4 re.
Gradual transition from 2/4 to 3/4.

74

Allegro molto: ($\dot{} = 116$)

80

III.

84

88